Ayrton

A Boy Who Loved Cars and Never Gave Up
on His Dreams

K.C YOUNGSTARS

THIS BOOK BELONGS TO

NAME:----------------------------

Born on March 21, 1960, in São Paulo, Brazil, Ayrton Senna wasn' just any ordinary guy

He became one of the fastest drivers
the world had ever seen!

AYRTON WAS KNOWN AS THE "RAIN MASTER" BECAUSE HE COULD DRIVE IN THE RAIN BETTER THAN ANYONE!

He was fearless, splashing through puddles and leaving the others in his dust!

In Brazil, Ayrton was more than just a race car driver; he was a superhero!

TABLE CONTENT

How Car Racing Started: A Funny Tale

A long, long time ago, way back when cars were brand new and still learning how to "vroom" down the road, people had an idea. These people looked at their cars and thought, "Hey, what if we tried racing these things?" But there was a problem… These cars were pretty slow. Some were so slow that if a squirrel ran by, the squirrel would win!

One day, two friends, Bob and Frank, decided to see who had the fastest car in their town. Now, Frank's car was red and shiny, while Bob's was blue and looked a bit like it was held together with chewing gum and a lot of hope. They lined up on a dirt road, counted to three, and off they went! Dust flew, chickens squawked, and people cheered as Bob and Frank "zoomed" down the street. At least, it felt like zooming to them.

The finish line was a giant potato sack at the end of the road. Frank was leading, but then his car made a strange "ker-plunk" sound, and it stopped right there in the middle of the road. Bob's car, held together by luck, wobbled right past Frank to the finish line! And just like that, Bob became the first race "champion" of the town.

After that day, people in towns all over wanted to race their cars. They started organizing races in open fields, on dirt tracks, and even on long stretches of road. The faster cars got, the more exciting the races became.

People loved watching them! It was like a rolling thunder of excitement, with cars whizzing past each other, sometimes so fast you couldn't see who was in the lead.

Eventually, car races became official, with tracks designed just for racing. These tracks were like roller coasters, full of twists, turns, and even loop-de-loops (okay, maybe not real loop-de-loops, but they felt like it!). Drivers wore cool suits, cars got painted in bright colors, and the crowds got bigger and bigger.

And that's how car racing was born! It started with two friends, a lot of dust, and a giant potato sack finish line. Now, it's a thrilling sport where the world's fastest cars race to see who's the best. But in the end, it's all about that same simple joy of driving fast and having fun. And maybe, just maybe, still trying to beat the squirrels!

CHAPTER 1:Who is Ayrton Senna?

Let's meet a real-life superhero of the racing world: Ayrton Senna! Born on March 21, 1960, in São Paulo, Brazil, Ayrton Senna wasn't just any ordinary guy. He became one of the fastest drivers the world had ever seen! But Ayrton wasn't only fast—he had a huge heart, tons of courage, and a love for his country that made him a hero to people everywhere.

Fun Facts About Ayrton Senna!

Zooming from a Young Age

Ayrton didn't wait to start his racing career! At just 4 years old, his father gave him a little go-kart. Ayrton was so tiny, he needed pillows to reach the pedals! But even as a kid, he showed his skills—he could zip and zoom like a pro.

The Rain Master

Ayrton was known as the "Rain Master" because he could drive in the rain better than anyone! While other drivers slowed down in wet weather, Ayrton flew around the track as if it was dry. He was fearless, splashing through puddles and leaving the others in his dust!

National Hero

In Brazil, Ayrton was more than just a race car driver; he was a superhero! He would wave the Brazilian flag every time he won a race, and everyone loved it. When he raced, people stopped what they were doing to watch. Shops closed, streets got quiet, and all eyes were on Ayrton as he made his country proud.

Kindness on Wheels

Ayrton cared deeply about others. He used his fame and fortune to help kids in Brazil, starting programs and donating money so that children could have better lives. He didn't just want to be the best on the track—he wanted to make the world a better place, too!

The Three-Time World Champion

Ayrton won the Formula One World Championship three times, in 1988, 1990, and 1991! His speed, skills, and bravery on the track made him a fan favorite. Everyone loved watching his daring moves and incredible driving.

A Racing Legend

Ayrton had a big rivalry with another famous driver named Alain Prost. It was one of the most exciting rivalries in racing history. They pushed each other to be better, and their races were always thrilling to watch!

Ayrton's Final Race and His Legacy

Sadly, Ayrton Senna's life ended during a race on May 1, 1994. He was doing what he loved most—racing—and people around the world mourned his loss. But Ayrton's legacy didn't stop there! To this day, people remember his bravery, kindness, and passion. The Ayrton Senna Institute was created to continue his work helping children in Brazil, and his story still inspires new drivers and fans all around the world.

Ayrton's Motto: "If You Have a Dream, Chase It!"

Ayrton Senna's life teaches us to dream big, never give up, and always try our best. Just like he chased his dreams at top speed, we can go after our dreams, too!

Whether it's on the track, in the classroom, or anywhere, Ayrton shows us that with courage and kindness, we can all make a difference.

CHAPTER 2:The Boy with a Need for Speed

Discovering Ayrton's Early Love for Racing
Once upon a time in Brazil, there was a little boy named Ayrton Senna who had a big, big dream! Ayrton wasn't like other kids. While his friends were playing soccer or hide-and-seek, Ayrton was already dreaming of speed, wheels, and zooming down a race track faster than anyone could imagine!
The Little Boy Who Loved Wheels
Ayrton's love for cars started before he could even say "vroom!" When he was just a toddler, he'd crawl over to his toy cars, push them around, and make all sorts of funny sounds. "Vroom-vroom! Zoom-zoom!" he'd say, pretending he was a race car driver. His parents noticed that little Ayrton seemed to be in his own world whenever he had a car toy in his hands. He'd be so focused, with his tiny eyebrows scrunched and his lips pressed together, as if he was racing for real!

The Big Surprise: A Tiny Car Just for Ayrton!

One day, when Ayrton was just 4 years old, his dad had a fantastic surprise for him—a go-kart! This wasn't a regular toy car; this was a real mini racing car that he could drive! Imagine how big his eyes got when he saw it! He couldn't believe his little dream car was actually real.

But wait—there was a problem! Ayrton was so small that his feet didn't reach the pedals! He tried stretching his legs out, but nope, he just couldn't reach. So, his dad had a clever idea. They grabbed a few pillows, stacked them on the seat, and ta-da! Ayrton could finally reach the pedals. He felt like the king of the road (or at least, the king of his backyard)!

The First Drive: Off Like a Rocket (Sort Of)

The moment Ayrton sat in his go-kart, he was ready to race. "Are you ready?" his dad asked. Ayrton nodded with a big grin. He gripped the steering wheel tightly, his heart beating with excitement. His dad gave him a gentle push, and off he went! Or at least… kind of. Ayrton's go-kart didn't exactly go "vroom" like he imagined; it sort of puttered and sputtered along. But Ayrton didn't mind—he was driving!

As he zipped around the yard, Ayrton started pretending he was in a big race, competing against the fastest drivers in the world. He'd make whooshing sounds and lean into the turns, feeling like a true racer. The flowers in the garden became his cheering fans, waving at him as he passed, and the trees stood tall like the crowd in a grand stadium. Ayrton was in his own little racecar world!

Speeding Up and Feeling the Thrill

Day after day, Ayrton practiced in his tiny go-kart. He went faster, learned to turn better, and even figured out how to make little drifts around corners. He felt the wind on his face, and it made him giggle. He loved the feeling of the wheels rolling beneath him and the sense that he could go anywhere.

Soon, Ayrton started racing his go-kart with his friends, and he almost always won! His friends would shout, "Hey, slow down, Ayrton!" But Ayrton didn't want to slow down—not one bit. He'd laugh and say, "Catch me if you can!" racing ahead with his arms waving like he was already a famous driver.

Racing Dreams Take Flight

As Ayrton grew, so did his dream of becoming a real racer. He practiced every chance he got, zooming around and imagining himself in a powerful, super-fast car. And do you know what? That little dream stuck with Ayrton for his whole life. He kept his love for racing close to his heart, and every time he sat behind the wheel, he felt that same excitement he'd had as a kid.

And that's how Ayrton Senna's racing story began— with a tiny go-kart, some pillows, and a big dream.

CHAPTER 3:Karting Adventures

Ayrton's Go-Kart Adventures: Where It All Began!
Ayrton Senna's love for racing didn't start in a fancy car or on a big, crowded racetrack. Nope! It all began with a little go-kart, and the excitement of zooming around on four wheels. You see, Ayrton's first "racing car" was tiny and simple, but to him, it was the greatest thing in the world!

The First Time Behind the Wheel
When Ayrton was just 4 years old, his dad surprised him with a go-kart. Now, this wasn't just any old go-kart. To little Ayrton, it was magic on wheels! Imagine the thrill of sitting in a tiny car that you could actually

drive! He was so small that he needed pillows to sit on, and his dad had to teach him how to press the pedals and turn the wheel. But Ayrton was a quick learner, and soon he was driving around as if he'd been born to race.

Falling in Love with Speed

As he grew older, Ayrton's go-karts got faster, and so did he! The first time he felt the wind whipping past his face, he knew there was something special about driving. He loved how he could turn corners just by tilting the wheel, and he felt powerful and free every time he picked up speed. Ayrton would race around his backyard, imagining he was competing in a big, exciting race. The flowers were his fans, and the garden was his race track. He'd say, "One day, I'll be the fastest!" And boy, did he mean it!

Why Ayrton Loved Go-Kart Racing

What made go-karting so magical for Ayrton? Here are a few reasons why he loved it so much:

Feeling Like a Hero

When Ayrton was behind the wheel, he felt like a superhero! The go-kart gave him the power to go fast, take sharp turns, and even drift a little. He loved feeling like he was in control, just him and the open track.

The Thrill of Speed

Ayrton loved how go-karting made his heart race! As he picked up speed, he felt a thrill that he couldn't get from anything else. The faster he went, the more alive he felt.

Learning New Skills

Go-karting wasn't just about speed; it was about skill, too. Ayrton loved the challenge of learning how to handle his kart. He practiced every chance he got, figuring out how to turn better, brake at the right time, and even outsmart other drivers.

The Spirit of Competition

As he got older, Ayrton began racing against other kids. He loved the excitement of trying to be the best!

Racing wasn't just about winning; it was about pushing himself to go faster, be braver, and learn more with each race.

A Dream in the Making

Go-karting made Ayrton feel like he was getting closer to his big dream. He didn't just want to be good—he wanted to be the best. Each time he raced, he felt like he was on a path that would lead him to greatness.

A Future Racing Star

Ayrton's love for go-karts grew with him, and he kept racing every chance he got. Go-karting wasn't just a hobby; it was where he learned the art of racing. The thrill of speed, the joy of competition, and the rush of taking on new challenges turned Ayrton from a little kid with a dream into a young racing star with big goals. He went from backyard races to big competitions, always with that same love and excitement for the track.

That's how Ayrton got his start in racing—with a go-kart, a lot of practice, and a love for the race that only grew stronger over time.

CHAPTER 4:The Road to Formula One

From Karting to the Fastest Cars in the World!
Imagine this: a young Ayrton Senna, zooming around in his little go-kart, making whooshing sounds and imagining he's the fastest driver on the planet. Well, it didn't stay a dream for long! Ayrton's talent, hard work, and love for speed would soon take him from backyard races to the biggest race tracks in the world.

The Beginning: Karting Superstar

As a kid, Ayrton spent hours racing his go-kart. He wasn't just having fun—he was getting really, really good! By the time he was 13 years old, Ayrton was racing in official go-kart competitions. And guess what? He started winning! His skills amazed everyone who watched, and people began to notice that this kid from Brazil wasn't just a regular racer—he had a natural gift for speed and control.

Going Global: Racing in Europe

Ayrton's dream kept growing, and soon he knew he had to race against the best. So, he traveled to Europe to compete in bigger karting championships. Ayrton faced off against the top young racers from around the world, and he quickly showed them what he could do. He won races, made friends (and rivals), and proved he could handle the pressure of big competitions.

But for Ayrton, karting was just the start. He wanted more. He dreamed of the world of Formula 1—the pinnacle of racing where only the fastest and best drivers got to compete. The engines were louder, the speeds were higher, and the cars were nothing like go-karts. But Ayrton was ready for the challenge.

Stepping Up: From Go-Karts to Formula Cars

After karting, Ayrton moved up to something faster: Formula Ford and Formula 3 racing. These cars were bigger, quicker, and way more powerful than go-karts. Ayrton had to learn new skills, like managing high-speed corners and understanding how to control a powerful car. But he loved every second of it. In no time, Ayrton was winning races in Formula Ford and Formula 3, just like he had with go-karts!

One of his most incredible victories came in Formula 3 at a track called Silverstone in England, where Ayrton raced against a fierce competitor named Martin Brundle. It was a thrilling battle, with both drivers pushing their cars to the limit. But Ayrton's determination shone through, and he won the championship! That win was like a golden ticket—it showed the world he was ready for Formula 1.

The Big Leap: Formula 1 Superstar

Finally, Ayrton got his chance to race in Formula 1, the highest level of racing in the world. He started with the Toleman team in 1984, and right away, he showed everyone he was a rising star. In a race in Monaco that year, it started raining, and Ayrton was in his element. He flew past driver after driver, almost winning the race. People couldn't believe how fast and fearless he was!

After that, Ayrton moved to Lotus, a famous racing team. It was with Lotus that he won his first Formula 1 race in 1985, and soon he was competing with the top drivers in the world, including his rival Alain Prost. Ayrton's driving style was unlike anyone else's—he was fast, daring, and wasn't afraid to take risks. The world watched in awe as he set records and won races.

Winning Championships and Becoming a Legend
In 1988, Ayrton joined McLaren, one of the best teams in Formula 1. That's when he truly became unstoppable. He went on to win three Formula 1 World Championships in 1988, 1990, and 1991. Ayrton didn't just race; he put on a show. Every race was a thrill ride, and every win felt like magic.

People called him "The Rain Master" because he could drive faster than anyone in wet conditions. He'd zoom through puddles and spray, leaving everyone in his wake. Fans cheered, and he became a national hero in Brazil. Whenever he won, he'd wave the Brazilian flag, making his country proud.

Ayrton Senna's Legacy: The Heart of a Champion

Ayrton Senna went from a boy in a go-kart to one of the greatest drivers in history, and he did it with courage, passion, and hard work. To this day, his story inspires racers and fans alike. Ayrton's journey shows that with determination, dreams really can come true. He showed the world that being a champion isn't just about speed—it's about heart, spirit, and the love of the race.

CHAPTER 5:The Rise of a Champion

Winning Races and Tackling Challenges!
Imagine you're Ayrton Senna, zooming down the track, wind whipping around you, the crowd cheering like crazy! But every race isn't easy. There are bumps, twists, fierce rivals, and even rainy weather to conquer. And that's exactly what Ayrton did—he took on every challenge and raced his heart out!
First Challenges in Formula 1
When Ayrton first joined Formula 1 in 1984, he was the new kid on the track. He started with a team called Toleman, and while they weren't the fastest team, Ayrton made sure everyone knew his name. He faced

some big challenges, like keeping up with faster cars and competing against top drivers who'd been racing for years. But Ayrton wasn't scared—he was ready to show his stuff.

One day, it started pouring rain at a famous track in Monaco, and the road turned super slippery. But Ayrton knew he could handle it! Rain made racing hard, but Ayrton loved it. He zoomed past other cars, slipping and sliding as he went, until he almost won! This race showed the world that Ayrton was one fearless racer who could handle any weather.

Moving to Lotus: The Quest for Speed

After his first year, Ayrton joined a team called Lotus. They had faster cars, and Ayrton couldn't wait to get behind the wheel. And guess what? In 1985, he won his first Formula 1 race in Portugal! The fans cheered, the cameras flashed, and Ayrton grinned from ear to ear. This win made him feel like a true champion, and he couldn't wait for more.

But with every race came new challenges. Sometimes his car had problems, or he'd face tough rivals who'd block him at every turn. But Ayrton kept pushing. He studied the tracks, practiced like crazy, and learned how to handle his car like a pro. He even became known as The Rain Master because of his amazing skills driving in wet weather. While other drivers slipped and struggled, Ayrton just got faster!

Joining McLaren: Racing with the Big Leagues

In 1988, Ayrton made a big move to McLaren, one of the best teams in Formula 1. This was his chance to go head-to-head with the fastest racers in the world. But there was one catch: his teammate, Alain Prost, was also one of the top drivers. And boy, did they become rivals! Every race turned into a battle between Ayrton and Alain, with both drivers fighting for the win.

They had some fierce races, where they'd race bumper-to-bumper, neither one giving an inch. Sometimes they'd even bump into each other (oops!), and sparks would fly! But Ayrton loved the challenge. Every time Alain sped up, Ayrton would find a way to go even faster. This rivalry pushed Ayrton to become an even better driver, and he was determined to come out on top.

Big Wins and Huge Celebrations

And did he ever! Ayrton won his first World Championship with McLaren in 1988. He was officially one of the best drivers in the world! But Ayrton didn't stop there. He kept winning races, setting records, and collecting trophies. His fans went wild, and he waved the Brazilian flag after each victory, showing his love for his home country.

The next few years were full of amazing wins, thrilling races, and more championships. Ayrton won three World Championships in total, in 1988, 1990, and 1991. Each time he won, it was a mix of excitement, hard work, and pride. Ayrton had gone from a kid in a go-kart to a world champion, and he did it by facing every challenge with courage and skill.

Ayrton's Legacy: A Champion of Heart

Ayrton's story is one of hard work, bravery, and a true love for racing. He wasn't just about speed—he was about never giving up, even when things got tough. Ayrton showed the world that a champion isn't just the one who crosses the finish line first; it's someone who faces every challenge with a big heart and an unstoppable spirit. And that's what made Ayrton Senna a true legend!

CHAPTER 6: Master of the Rain

Why Ayrton Was Called the "Rain Master"

Imagine you're at a Formula 1 race. It's pouring rain, the track is slippery, and drivers are struggling just to stay on the road. Most drivers slow down, gripping the steering wheel tight, hoping they don't slide off the track. But not Ayrton Senna! When it rained, Ayrton became a whole different racer—faster, sharper, and almost unstoppable. That's why people started calling him the "Rain Master."

Mastering the Art of Rain Racing

For Ayrton, rain wasn't a problem; it was an adventure! He had this amazing ability to control his car in wet conditions like no other driver. While other cars would slide or even spin out of control, Ayrton seemed to glide through the rain like he was racing on a sunny day. He knew how to read the track, find the driest spots, and make quick decisions to stay in control.

One of Ayrton's most famous races in the rain was the 1984 Monaco Grand Prix. It was only his first season in Formula 1, and he was driving a slower car with the Toleman team. But when it started raining, Ayrton went into full Rain Master mode! He zoomed past car after car, catching up with even the fastest drivers. By the time the race was stopped because of the rain,

Ayrton had gone from 13th place to 2nd! The crowd couldn't believe it, and the nickname "Rain Master" began to stick.

Why Was Ayrton So Good in the Rain?

What made Ayrton so good in the rain? It wasn't magic—it was a mix of skill, bravery, and a deep understanding of his car. Here's what helped him:

Sharp Reflexes: Ayrton had lightning-fast reflexes. When racing in the rain, every second counts. He knew exactly when to turn the wheel, hit the brakes, or speed up, all in the blink of an eye!

Fearless Spirit: Racing in the rain is scary. The car can slide, and crashes are more likely. But Ayrton wasn't scared. He saw the rain as his time to shine. His fearless attitude made him brave enough to take risks that other drivers wouldn't dare.

Amazing Control: Ayrton knew his car inside and out. He knew how much to press the gas, how hard to brake, and how to steer just right so the car didn't slide out. In the rain, he handled the car as if it was an extension of himself.

Focus and Confidence: When it rained, Ayrton was laser-focused. He believed in his skills and trusted his instincts. He knew that if he kept his focus, he could handle anything, even the wildest rainstorm.

More Rainy Victories

Throughout his career, Ayrton proved again and again that he was the Rain Master. In 1993, at the European Grand Prix in Donington Park, England, it was another wet race. On the first lap alone, Ayrton passed four cars in just a few turns, taking the lead like a true champion. The rain didn't slow him down—it made him faster!

Fans loved watching Ayrton race in the rain. They'd cheer extra loud, knowing they were about to see something incredible. For Ayrton, rainy races were a chance to show off his special skills and prove to the world that he was more than just fast—he was a true master of the track, rain or shine. And that's how he earned his legendary title: the Rain Master!

CHAPTER 7:Rivalries and Friendships

Ayrton's Rivals and Friends: Racing with Legends!

Ayrton Senna didn't just race against any ordinary drivers; he competed with some of the biggest names in Formula 1! These racers were fast, skilled, and determined to win. Along the way, Ayrton made a few friends and, yes, some serious rivals too! Let's meet some of the famous drivers he raced against and the friendships he built.

Alain Prost: The Fierce Rival

First up is Alain Prost, a French driver with incredible speed and skill. Ayrton and Alain were like fire and ice on the track—two top drivers with completely different styles. Alain was known as "The Professor" because he liked to plan his races and drive smart, while Ayrton relied on his instincts and took big risks. The two raced each other fiercely, especially when they both drove for McLaren. They pushed each other to the limit, each one trying to be faster than the other. Sometimes, they would even bump into each other in their battles for the win! Their rivalry was so intense that fans around the world would cheer extra loud when they were on the track together. But here's the twist: even though they were rivals, deep down, they respected each other. Years later, they became friends, showing that true sportsmanship can bring people together.

Gerhard Berger: The Best Buddy

While Ayrton and Alain were rivals, Ayrton found a great friend in Gerhard Berger, an Austrian driver. Gerhard and Ayrton drove together at McLaren, and they quickly became best buds. They were always laughing and pulling pranks on each other. Once, Gerhard even filled Ayrton's hotel room with frogs as a joke!

On the track, Gerhard and Ayrton respected each other's skills and raced fairly. Off the track, they had tons of fun together, which made the races even more enjoyable. Gerhard helped Ayrton relax and have fun, and he always had Ayrton's back. Even though they were competitors, their friendship stayed strong, and they shared some unforgettable moments.

Nelson Piquet: The Brazilian Rival

Ayrton also raced against Nelson Piquet, another famous Brazilian driver. Since they were both from Brazil, people naturally compared them, and their rivalry was strong. Nelson was already a champion when Ayrton joined Formula 1, and he wasn't too thrilled about sharing the spotlight with another Brazilian.

The two had some intense races, but they brought out the best in each other. While they didn't always get along, Ayrton and Nelson showed the world that Brazil had some of the fastest drivers ever!

Nigel Mansell: The Fearless Brit

Another famous driver Ayrton raced against was Nigel Mansell from the United Kingdom. Known for his bravery and determination, Nigel was one of the few drivers who could match Ayrton's fierce driving style. When Ayrton and Nigel raced together, it was like watching two lions fighting for the top spot!

One of their most famous moments was in 1992 at the Monaco Grand Prix, where Nigel chased Ayrton for lap after lap. Nigel was right behind him, trying to pass, but Ayrton blocked every move like a pro. In the end, Ayrton held onto his lead and won the race, but the two gave each other a respectful nod. Even though they were rivals, they shared a mutual respect for each other's skills.

Making Friends Along the Way

Racing isn't just about winning; it's also about meeting people who share the same passion. Ayrton's kindness and charm made him a popular figure in the racing world. He inspired many young drivers, showing them how to race with courage and heart.

He also made friends outside the track. People loved Ayrton for his caring personality. He donated money to help the poor in Brazil, and his heart was as big as his love for racing. Ayrton was more than just a champion—he was a friend to many and a hero to fans around the world.

Ayrton's Legacy: Rivals and Friends

Through rivalries, friendships, pranks, and respect, Ayrton's journey showed that racing is more than just speed—it's about passion, courage, and sometimes a bit of fun along the way. His story teaches us that even when we compete, we can make friends, respect each other, and cheer each other on. Ayrton's rivals pushed him to be the best, and his friends made every race a special memory.

CHAPTER 8:Racing for Brazil

In the vibrant city of São Paulo, Brazil, a young boy named Ayrton Senna dreamed of speed and adventure. From the very beginning, Ayrton was captivated by the thrill of racing. He loved to watch cars zoom past and imagined himself behind the wheel, feeling the rush of wind against his face. His family noticed his passion and encouraged him to pursue it, which set him on a remarkable path.

As a child, Ayrton's first taste of racing came when he hopped into a go-kart. With his tiny hands gripping the steering wheel, he zipped around the track, feeling the excitement surge through him. Every time he raced, he felt alive. He practiced tirelessly, mastering every twist and turn, and soon he was winning local races. His family and friends cheered him on, believing he was destined for greatness.

When Ayrton was a teenager, he took a bold step and moved to Europe to chase his dream of becoming a professional race car driver. It was a big leap, filled with challenges and new experiences. He competed in various racing championships, where he faced tough opponents. But Ayrton was not one to back down. He trained hard, learned from his experiences, and kept pushing himself to be better.

His big break came when he joined the Formula One racing world, the most exciting and competitive form of car racing. Ayrton's debut was filled with nerves, excitement, and a strong desire to prove himself. With his incredible talent and determination, he quickly became a force to be reckoned with on the racetrack. He dazzled fans with his skills, and each race brought him closer to his dream of becoming a world champion.

In 1988, Ayrton achieved his first major victory, winning his first Formula One World Championship. The news spread like wildfire across Brazil. People poured into the streets, waving flags and celebrating their hero. Ayrton had not just won a trophy; he had brought immense joy and pride to his country. He became a symbol of hope and inspiration for many, especially children who dreamed of following in his footsteps.

Ayrton's incredible talent on the racetrack was matched only by his love for his country. He wore the Brazilian flag on his racing suit with pride, showing everyone that he was racing for Brazil. When he won, it felt like the whole nation had won together. The joy and excitement he brought to his fans were palpable, and they adored him for it.

But Ayrton's journey was not just about winning races. He believed in using his success to make a difference. He started a charity to help children in Brazil, providing them with educational opportunities and healthcare. He wanted every child to have a chance to follow their dreams, just like he had. Ayrton visited schools, met with young athletes, and shared his story, inspiring countless kids to believe in themselves and work hard.

Throughout his career, Ayrton faced many challenges, including fierce rivalries on the racetrack. But he always handled them with grace and sportsmanship.

He respected his competitors and understood that racing was not just about winning but also about the love of the sport. This attitude earned him respect from fans and fellow drivers alike.

Tragically, Ayrton's life was cut short during a race in Italy. The news of his accident shocked the world, and his fans mourned the loss of their beloved champion.

But even in his absence, Ayrton's legacy continued to shine brightly. His spirit of determination, kindness, and passion for racing inspired new generations of drivers and fans.

Today, Ayrton Senna is celebrated as a national hero in Brazil. Statues and murals of him adorn public spaces, reminding everyone of his incredible achievements.

Races are held in his honor, and young drivers continue to aspire to be like him. Ayrton taught the world that with passion, hard work, and a big heart, anything is possible. His story encourages kids everywhere to dream big, work hard, and make a positive impact on their communities.

So, the next time you watch a race or see a fast car zooming by, remember Ayrton Senna, the boy from Brazil who became a racing legend and a symbol of hope for so many. His journey shows that with courage and determination, you can overcome any obstacle and inspire others along the way.

CHAPTER 9:Tragic Day at Imola

Ayrton Senna's final race was held on May 1, 1994, at the Imola circuit in Italy. It was a day that started like any other for the Formula One legend, but it would end in tragedy and change the world of racing forever. The weekend had already been marked by a series of unfortunate events, including the fatal crash of Ayrton's friend and fellow driver, Roland Ratzenberger, just one day before. The atmosphere at the track was heavy with sadness and concern, but

Ayrton, being the passionate racer he was, was determined to compete.

As the race began, Ayrton's skill and determination were on full display. He was in the lead and seemed poised for victory. However, just a few laps into the race, tragedy struck. As he approached a high-speed corner called Tamburello, Ayrton's car went off track and crashed into a concrete wall at an incredible speed.

Despite the medical team's swift response, Ayrton suffered severe head injuries and was pronounced dead shortly after the crash.

The news of Ayrton's death shocked the world. Fans, fellow drivers, and racing officials were devastated. Ayrton was not just a champion on the racetrack; he was a hero to many. His passion for racing, his kindness, and his dedication to helping others had left a lasting impression on everyone who knew him or followed his career.

In the aftermath of his death, there was a global outpouring of grief. Millions mourned the loss of a legend, and his funeral in São Paulo drew thousands of fans and admirers, who came to pay their respects. People remembered Ayrton not just for his incredible achievements in Formula One but also for the way he carried himself, his dedication to his country, and his commitment to giving back to the community.

Ayrton's legacy extended far beyond his racing accolades. His tragic passing prompted significant changes in the sport of Formula One. The racing community rallied together to address safety concerns that had been long overdue. New regulations were implemented to improve car safety, and circuits underwent redesigns to reduce risks for drivers. Ayrton's death served as a wake-up call that transformed the sport, making it safer for future generations of racers.

Beyond racing, Ayrton Senna became a symbol of hope and inspiration. His charity work, which focused on helping children in Brazil, continued to thrive after his death. The Ayrton Senna Institute was established to honor his memory, providing educational opportunities for underprivileged children and ensuring that Ayrton's dream of helping others lived on. The foundation has touched the lives of countless young people, empowering them to pursue their dreams, just as he had done.

Today, Ayrton Senna is remembered not just as one of the greatest drivers in Formula One history but as a beloved national hero in Brazil. His story is taught in schools, and his legacy continues to inspire young athletes around the world. Statues, murals, and monuments dedicated to him can be found in many places, celebrating the life of a man who transcended racing and became a beacon of hope for many. Ayrton Senna taught us that life is precious, and pursuing our passions with dedication and heart can make a difference in the world. His final race serves as a reminder of the fragility of life and the importance of safety, while his legacy lives on in the hearts of those he inspired. So whenever you see a race or hear his name, remember Ayrton Senna—the brave racer who became a legend and whose impact will be felt for generations to come.

CHAPTER 10:The Legend Lives On

Ayrton Senna is remembered today as one of the greatest Formula One drivers of all time, and his legacy continues to inspire millions around the world. His life story is not just about his incredible racing skills; it's about his character, his passion for the sport, and his commitment to making a difference in the lives of others. Here's a look at how Ayrton is remembered and why he remains a source of inspiration today.

1. A Legend on the Track

Ayrton Senna's achievements on the racetrack are nothing short of legendary. He won three Formula One World Championships and secured numerous victories, with 41 Grand Prix wins. His unmatched skill, fierce determination, and remarkable ability to push the limits of speed captivated fans and fellow drivers alike. Many remember his breathtaking performances, especially his incredible rain driving skills and his famous battles with rivals, showcasing not just his talent but also his passion for racing.

2. Safety Advocate

Following his tragic accident in 1994, Ayrton's legacy took on a new dimension. His death served as a catalyst for significant changes in Formula One racing. His passing highlighted the urgent need for improved safety measures, leading to the introduction of new regulations regarding car designs, track safety, and medical protocols. Today, drivers benefit from the advancements made in safety technology, which has saved countless lives. Ayrton's commitment to safety has left a lasting impact on the sport, ensuring that future generations of drivers can compete in a safer environment.

3. Philanthropic Legacy

Ayrton was not only a champion on the racetrack but also a champion for children in need. He founded the Ayrton Senna Institute, a charitable organization dedicated to providing education and support for underprivileged children in Brazil. The institute has helped millions of children gain access to quality education and has empowered them to achieve their dreams. His commitment to helping others is a central part of his legacy, and the institute continues to honor his memory by transforming lives and fostering hope.

4. Cultural Icon

In Brazil, Ayrton Senna is more than just a racing legend; he is a cultural icon. His story is celebrated in books, documentaries, and films that capture his journey from a young boy in São Paulo to a global superstar. Statues and murals in his honor can be found throughout Brazil, and his face adorns countless memorabilia. He is celebrated as a national hero, and his impact goes beyond racing, making him a beloved figure in Brazilian culture.

5. Inspiring Future Generations

Ayrton Senna's story continues to inspire young athletes and aspiring racers around the world. His journey teaches valuable lessons about perseverance, dedication, and the importance of following one's passion. Young drivers look up to him not only for his incredible racing achievements but also for his character and sportsmanship. Ayrton's ability to overcome challenges and his commitment to his dreams resonate with people of all ages, encouraging them to strive for greatness in their own lives.

6. Celebrated Anniversaries and Events

Every year, fans around the world come together to celebrate Ayrton Senna's life and legacy. Special events, races, and tributes are held in his honor, including the annual Ayrton Senna Race, where young kart drivers pay tribute to him by competing in his name. These gatherings keep his memory alive, reminding everyone of the joy he brought to racing and the inspiration he continues to provide.

7. Emotional Impact

Ayrton Senna's life story touches the hearts of many. His passion for racing, his kindness towards others, and his unwavering determination serve as powerful reminders of the impact one person can have on the world. His struggles and triumphs resonate with people facing their own challenges, reminding them that success often comes from hard work and resilience. Ayrton Senna is remembered as a racing legend, a safety advocate, a philanthropist, and a cultural icon. His legacy continues to inspire new generations of athletes and fans, encouraging them to chase their dreams while making a positive difference in the world. Ayrton's story is a testament to the power of passion, perseverance, and compassion, and it will continue to inspire for years to come.

CHAPTER 11:Fun Facts and Quiz Time

Fun Facts About Ayrton Senna

Early Start: Ayrton started karting at just 7 years old, quickly showcasing his talent and love for racing. Winning Streak: He won his first Formula One World Championship in 1988, and he was known for his incredible performance in wet conditions, often winning races in the rain.

Brazilian Pride: Ayrton was extremely proud of his Brazilian heritage and often displayed the Brazilian flag on his race car and racing suit.

Rivalry with Alain Prost: Ayrton had a famous rivalry with fellow driver Alain Prost. Their fierce competition created some of the most exciting moments in Formula One history.

Philanthropist: Ayrton founded the Ayrton Senna Institute, which focuses on providing education and opportunities for underprivileged children in Brazil.

Safety Changes: After his tragic accident in 1994, many safety improvements were made in Formula One, directly influencing the sport's regulations and car designs.

Cultural Icon: In Brazil, Ayrton Senna is considered a national hero, and his legacy continues to inspire many through statues, documentaries, and books.

Record-Breaker: At the time of his retirement in 1994, Ayrton held the record for the most pole positions in Formula One, with 65.

Quiz Questions About Ayrton Senna

What age did Ayrton Senna start karting?

a) 5 years old

b) 7 years old

c) 10 years old

Which year did Ayrton win his first Formula One World Championship?

---

a) 1985

b) 1988

c) 1991

What was Ayrton Senna known for excelling in?

---

a) Racing on sunny days

b) Racing in rainy conditions

c) Off-road racing

Who was Ayrton's main rival during his racing career?

---

a) Nigel Mansell

b) Alain Prost

c) Michael Schumacher

What organization did Ayrton establish to help children in Brazil?

---

a) Ayrton Senna Foundation

b) Ayrton Senna Institute

c) Ayrton Senna Charity

What significant change occurred in Formula One after Ayrton's death?

---

a) Changes to the rules on tire colors

b) Improvements in car safety regulations

c) Introduction of new racing tracks

In how many Formula One World Championships did Ayrton Senna win?

---

a) 1

b) 2

c) 3

What did Ayrton often display on his racing suit to show his pride for his country?

---

a) The Brazilian flag

b) The Formula One logo

c) His own picture

Answers to the Quiz Questions

b) **7 years old**

b) 1988

b) Racing in rainy conditions

b) Alain Prost

b) Ayrton Senna Institute

b) Improvements in car safety regulations

c) 3

a) The Brazilian flag

<u>Activities!!</u>

ANSWER KEY

	3
	6
	2
	4
	5

EASTER DECORATION

Decorate and color your Easter egg.

Shadow Matching

Draw a line between each car element and it's shadow.

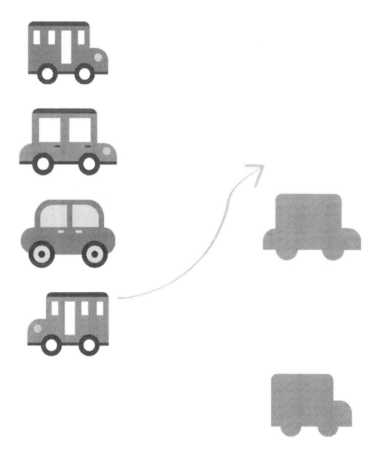

CONCLUSION

Once upon a time in Brazil, there was a little boy named Ayrton Senna who had a big dream—he wanted to become a racing superstar! From the moment he got his first go-kart at just 7 years old, Ayrton zoomed around the track with a huge smile on his face, and everyone could see that he was born to race! As he grew up, Ayrton raced in many competitions and became a champion in karting, winning races left and right. His passion for speed was contagious, and soon he caught the attention of the big leagues—Formula One! In 1984, he got his chance to race with the best drivers in the world, and he was off to the races! Ayrton quickly became known for his incredible skills on the track. He loved racing in the rain, which was unusual because most drivers found it tricky. But Ayrton was like a superhero, zipping around corners while others struggled. In 1988, he achieved his dream by winning his first Formula One World Championship. He was so happy that he waved the

Brazilian flag proudly, making his country cheer with joy!

But it wasn't just about winning for Ayrton. He had a big heart and cared deeply for the people around him. He used his fame to help children in Brazil through his charity, the Ayrton Senna Institute, providing education and support to those in need. He believed that every child should have the chance to chase their dreams, just like he did!

Ayrton had a famous rival, Alain Prost, and their exciting races were like watching a thrilling adventure movie! They would race neck and neck, pushing each other to be better. Fans loved the excitement of their competition, and it made Ayrton even more determined to win.

However, in 1994, during a race in Italy, something very sad happened. Ayrton had a terrible accident, and even though he was a superhero on the track, he could not escape this time. The world was heartbroken. People all over Brazil mourned the loss of their hero, and the racing community came together to remember him.

After his passing, many changes were made to make racing safer, ensuring that future drivers could enjoy the sport he loved without taking unnecessary risks. Ayrton's legacy lived on, and his story inspired a new generation of racers and fans.

Today, Ayrton Senna is remembered not just as a champion racer but as a caring hero who showed us all the importance of following our dreams, helping others, and racing with passion. His incredible journey from a small boy with a dream to a global icon continues to inspire kids everywhere to chase their own dreams and make a difference in the world. And that, dear friends, is the amazing story of Ayrton Senna!

Glossary

Ayrton Senna: A famous Brazilian race car driver known for his incredible skills in Formula One racing and his big heart for helping others.

Racing: A sport where drivers compete to see who can go the fastest around a track in specially designed cars.

Go-Kart: A small, lightweight racing car that is often used by kids and beginners to learn how to race.

Formula One (F1): The highest class of single-seater auto racing in the world, featuring fast cars and exciting races held on special tracks.

Champion: A person who wins first place in a competition; a winner!

Pole Position: The starting position at the front of the grid for the driver who qualifies fastest for a race.

Competitor: A person or team that takes part in a contest or race against others.

Rival: A person or team that competes against someone else; a competitor who is often seen as a challenge.

Legacy: Something that is left behind after someone is gone; the impact and memory a person leaves for others.

Philanthropist: A person who helps others by donating time, money, or resources to make a positive change in the world.

Charity: An organization that helps people in need or supports a good cause, often through donations and fundraising.

Institute: An organization or establishment created for a specific purpose, such as education or research.

Safety Regulations: Rules put in place to keep people safe while doing an activity, like racing.

Heartbroken: Feeling very sad because of a loss or a tragedy.

Inspiration: A person or thing that motivates others to do something great or to pursue their dreams.

Hero: A person admired for their courage, outstanding achievements, or noble qualities; someone who inspires others.

Determination: The quality of being firm and strong in your purpose; not giving up easily.

Adventure: An exciting experience or journey, often filled with challenges and new discoveries.

Superstar: A very famous and successful person, especially in sports or entertainment.

National Pride: A feeling of satisfaction and pride in one's country and its achievements.

Made in the USA
Las Vegas, NV
09 November 2024

11454300R00033